T0158974

I Loved Them First

Karen Phelps

Inspiring Voices®
A Service of **Guideposts**

Inspiring Voices books may be ordered through booksellers or by contacting:

Inspiring Voices
1663 Liberty Drive
Bloomington, IN 47403
www.inspiringvoices.com
1-(866) 697-5313

Because of the dynamic nature of the Internet, any web addresses or links contained in this book may have changed since publication and may no longer be valid. The views expressed in this work are solely those of the author and do not necessarily reflect the views of the publisher, and the publisher hereby disclaims any responsibility for them.

Any people depicted in stock imagery provided by Thinkstock are models, and such images are being used for illustrative purposes only.

Certain stock imagery © Thinkstock.

ISBN: 978-1-4624-0333-2 (sc)
ISBN: 978-1-4624-0332-5 (e)

Library of Congress Control Number: 2012918608

Printed in the United States of America

Inspiring Voices rev. date: 10/03/2012

Dedication

To Lady, who guided and protected me through childhood, adolescence and into my twenties.
To all the collies of Karenthia who followed her.
To Rufus and Keri who continue to teach me.

"Whenever man gets into trouble, God sends a dog."

—Alphonese Toussenel

Contents

List of Photographs

Cover - Karen, Juliet and Lady
     Photographer: Karen Pilzer

Photo 1 - Mayona on Trigger
     Photographer: Ralph Emerson Mayers

Photo 2 – Karen on Stick Horse with Mayona
     Photographer: Louise Phelps

Photo 3 – Karen on Golden Boy
     Photographer: Ralph Emerson Mayers

Photo 4 - Karen on Juliet
     Photographer: Karen Pilzer

Photo 5 – Lady (head study)
     Photographer: Karen Phelps

Photo 6 – Karen (age 13) and Lady
     Photographer: Ralph Emerson Mayers

Photo 7 – Splash and littermates
     Photographer: Karen Phelps

Photo 8 – Cindy (head study)
     Photographer: Karen Phelps

Photo 9 – Kieno (head study)
     Photographer: Karen Phelps

Photo 10 – Karen with lap full of puppies
     Photographer: Celeste Kolb

Photo 11 – Karen and Terra-Cotta (as puppy)
     Photographer: Louise Phelps

Photo 12 – Bobby (head study)
     Photographer: Ralph Emerson Mayers

Photo 13 – Travis (sitting)
     Photographer: Karen Phelps

Photo 14 – Karen and Lady on the beach
     Photographer: Mayona Phelps

Acknowledgements

Grateful thanks to Karen Pilzer, Lorraine Ash, Roberta Gardner, Jean Reid, Jo Ann Clark, Karen Rippstein, and my sister, Mayona Phelps Engdahl, for editing, helpful comments, and cheering me on.

I Loved Them First

Sometimes
I close my eyes
and see horses
as far as the eye can see.
I loved them first.

As a little girl
if I could have found a way
I'd have ridden off
and never come back.
I would have made horses
my whole existence.

I'd be riding still
on pintos or palominos,
on buckskins or blood bays,
with gypsies or cowboys,
with the circus or a stable,
I'd be jumping or racing,
cutting cattle or teaching lessons.

Sometimes
I close my eyes
and see horses
as far as the eye can see.

I loved them first.

Black Wind

The painting of the black horse grabs me.
I'd recognize him anywhere.
It is Black Wind,
the stallion of my childhood.
He is large and untamed
yet gentle and obedient.
He loves only me.
I close my eyes
and summon him.

My hands feel the ripple of muscles
beneath his sloping shoulder.
I stroke his velvet nose
feel the breath from his nostrils
blow hot and wet
in my cupped hand.
The course hair of his mane
covers me as I throw
my arms around him.
Resting my cheek
against his glossy neck,
I inhale the familiar perfume of horse.
I listen to his proud heart
pumping blood through his veins,
the thundering sound of air
rushing into his lungs.
My face warms from his heat.

Black Wind
is a magic name,
an incantation.
He stole my heart long ago.
After all these years
he still takes my breath away.

Something deep within me responds
to his wild, black horse.

A childhood longing is reawakened
like a sleeper from a dream;
a long-forgotten passion is recalled
like an old sailor remembers the sea.

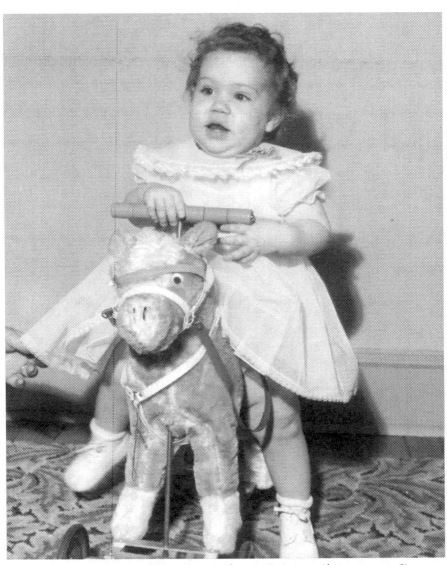

My baby sister, Mayona , (9 months) on Trigger (Christmas 1956)

Trigger

The Christmas I was five
Santa brought Trigger
a golden pony on red wheels
a miniature version of
Roy Rogers' famous palomino
I watched every week on TV.

Trigger wore a white plastic bridle
and a red leather saddle.
I was too big to ride him though
and had to settle for wheeling
my dolls around on his back.

Only my baby sister
was small enough to ride him.
I hated her
for riding *my* pony.

My mother didn't understand
she waved aside my protests.
It took me years to love my sister
and decades to really appreciate her.

Karen on stick horse (Black Wind) with Mayona and black
lab, Joe, in Lanark, Ontario, Canada – 1960

Horse Crazy

Grandma said my love of horses
came from her side of the family.
She told stories of her brothers
racing swift black horses
over the frozen lakes in Finland.
One birthday she embroidered
two horses for me:
one black, the other a palomino.
I loved her understanding of my passion.
Her pictures still hang in my bedroom.

I asked for a pony
every Christmas and birthday.
I loved horses with the intensity
and steadfast devotion of a child.

My mother made me a stick horse
from black satin with a rabbit fur mane.
I jumped Black Wind over fences
made of bean poles from Dad's garden.
I knew where every horse lived
along the roads we traveled.

Saturday mornings
astride my stick horse
I'd watch "Fury" on TV
about a boy and the black horse he loved.

At school I'd gallop around the playground
with a jump rope around my waist
while someone held the reins behind.
There was a herd of horse-mad girls
to play horses with at recess.

Karen (age 7) riding Golden Boy - 1958

Golden Boy

When I was seven
God answered my prayers.
Our next door neighbors
kept a horse for the summer
a big, gentle palomino named Golden Boy.
I lived in their yard.
We brushed him and fed him and walked him
inhaling his pungent horse smell.
We spent hours watching him eat grass
while he switched his tail and
stamped his large hooves at the flies.
We worshipped at the feet
of this big, golden god.

Uncle Em photographed me riding him.
Though the photo is in black and white,
I remember my shorts were blue
and my sneakers red.
I sit on a plaid blanket instead of a saddle
bare-chested with a hint of breasts to come.
My hair is long and braided
my bangs cut unbecomingly short.
I hold the reins with my left hand
and his blonde mane with my right.

My smile is sweet and proud.
"Do you see me?" it asks
"Do you see me riding this horse all by
myself?"
I sit tall and powerful
astride this beautiful palomino.
I made my dream come true
wished it into being.

Faster, Faster

I loved horses.
I loved the pungent smell of
horse hair, sweat and fresh hay.
I loved the rich smell of saddles
and the feel of boots well broken in.
I loved cleaning bridles
with sponges and saddle soap.
I loved holding thick leather reins
while the horses stamped their feet and
clanked the bit against their teeth.
I loved walking them in blankets to cool.
I loved brushing them until
my arms ached and their coats shone.

I loved their size.
I loved their power.
I loved their danger.

When I was riding
I couldn't think about anything
except a thousand pounds
of horse flesh moving beneath me.
Riding was the ultimate escape.
It made me feel powerful.
It made me feel beautiful.
It made me feel whole.
It made me feel like a goddess.

One week in January I went to the stables
ill tempered and out of sorts.
The temperatures dropped below zero.
The wind blew hard and cold
freezing everything in its path.
I was sick to death of winter.

No one showed up in my class.
I trotted briskly around the ring alone

trying to keep warm on Juliet
a slim, bay thoroughbred.
She was so sweet tempered
even the smallest child could ride her.
She had a classic head
and a soft, alert expression.
My hands were light and
Juliet was always willing for me.
An ex-race horse, she was nearly 17 hands
and she was my favorite horse.

Juliet hadn't been exercised in three days.
She kept poking her head out arching her back
and giving me an uncomfortable ride.
No matter what I did
she fought to stretch her head out
as if she were out of sorts, too.

We trotted in both directions
and settled down into a quiet canter.
Then, Roxanne asked me to gallop.
I'd never galloped a horse before.
I was scared.

I urged Juliet forward.
She was hesitant at first
then responded to my coaxing.
Her well-bred legs stretched out.
Her stride lengthened.
Her hooves became louder and louder
as our speed increased.
The wind picked up.
We cantered faster and faster
deep into the corners.
The dirt flew up behind us.
The ground blurred beneath me.
Juliet strained against the bit.
I struggled to hold her in check.

Karen riding Juliet – 1975

"Let her out," Roxanne yelled.
"Let her run."

I released Juliet.
Her regal neck stretched out
while I balanced like a jockey over her neck
struggling to keep my balance.
The turns came quicker and quicker.
I sat down in the corners making her slow up.
On the stretches I urged her flat out.
Juliet gathered more speed.
The wind made my face burn
and my eyes squint.
Her hooves pounded
faster than my own heartbeats.
Around and around
faster and faster we flew.
We were moving so fast
it seemed we were in slow motion.
The air rushed past blocking all sound
except my breath and Juliet under me.
Faster, faster, faster.
Her long, graceful legs
rejoiced in the motion of running.
This was what she was bred for.
This was what she loved to do.
This was what she knew best.
Perched precariously on her back
I shared in her love of running.
I knew the primeval joy the Scythians
and Apaches felt riding horses
instead of walking upon the earth.

The wind squeezed tears from my eyes
and the thundering of Juliet's hooves
muffled my sobs as I wept
from the sheer beauty of it.
There was no separation
Between me and the thoroughbred I straddled.

Time had stopped.
We were in suspended animation.
My spirit soared as she hurtled me
into another space and time.
It was a bonding and a fusion.
It was communication on such a deep level
that the horse beneath me responded
before she was asked.
It was a communion of spirit, of joy, of speed.
I had known in my soul since childhood
that riding would be like this.
For one brief moment
tearing around the ring at breakneck speed
I knew perfection.

Yardstick

For a year I begged my parents for a dog.
They gave in and my mother located a litter
whose grandmother was a pure-bred collie.
I chose the only buff-colored one
among her black littermates.
I named her Lady.

She became my companion, my protector, my friend.
I trained her to obey hand signals, whistles and voice.
She retrieved my slippers, carried notes,
then trained all the collies who came after her.
Anyone who met Lady wanted a dog just like her.

I knew nothing of death in those years.
I was seven when Grandpa Fiedler died.
We weren't allowed at his funeral.
My cousin, Shaver,
came home from Vietnam
in a body bag.
I'd wanted to marry him when I was little
until he told me first cousins couldn't.
Everyone in town came to pay their respects,
even Mr.Pine, the assistant principal,
who always gave him detention.

No one in my family understood
why I went to a dog show the day after the funeral.
How could I explain the solace dogs gave me?
I didn't understand it myself back then.
Mother disapproved of the garish trophy
Bobby brought home that day.
It was as if her displeasure cursed him.
His nerves couldn't take the show ring
and my dreams of his championship ended,
along with his promising show career.
Eventually he came to live with Lady and me

My beloved first dog, Lady

at my Cross River apartment.
Then, while I was away, Lady got sick,
and I rushed home to visit her at the vet's.
Too weak to stand,
she wagged her tail in greeting
from the stainless steel table she lay on.
She kissed my hand to comfort me
as I sobbed into her ruff.
Finally, she let out a long, deep sigh.
Lady knew this was good-bye.

Lady's death became the yardstick
of all my future grief.
Neither a long, bitter divorce
nor the death of my father
has equaled the heartbreak
of her passing.

Karen (age 13) and Lady (2 ½ years old) - 1964

The Gift

Lady was leery of my father.
Was it the beer on his breath
or his loud, gruff, voice?

Sometimes he fell asleep on the sofa
then sat up, groggy and looked around.
She growled softly
until he stumbled off to bed,
protecting me
from what she considered
potential harm.

He built her kennel run
from welded scraps of steel,
the unspoken acceptance
of this dog of mine.

Lady became a celebrity
when his friends stopped by
and I demonstrated her tricks.
They all wanted a dog like her
as if you could pick one
like an apple, off a tree.

One night my father brought home a leash
he'd made from braided nylon cord.
Shyly I accepted the gift,
unused to his attention,
amazed he'd taken the time
to make it just for me.

Lady has long since passed away
and my father's been dead five years,
yet I still have the nylon leash
he made all those years ago.

My fourth litter – 1983. Splash is on right in front.

Pick of the Litter

How do you choose the best puppy?
Wendy's pups are five weeks old and
hang out of the yellow laundry basket
in the bright sun on green grass.
Mom's hand on the side steadies them
while I take the photo.
I made a noise and they all look at me.
It's chaos, frozen in time
the present and future collide
in this colored photograph.

I kept the sable pup on the right
a big, bold, beautiful bitch
with a splash of white on her brown neck
first to climb out of the brood box
with personality to burn.
No one who saw the litter understood
what I saw in her.
They were blinded by her flashy littermates
and their full, white collars.
I saw beyond the nondescript markings
and recognized my destiny
in the depths of her amber eyes.

Splash became the mother of
Travis, Terra-Cotta, Spitfire and Sassafrass.
Coupled with her mother,
she won Best Herding Brace
at the Ramapo Kennel Club show
and shared my life for twelve years.
She was my pick of the litter.
I made the right choice.

Cindy – Carwill's Witch of Karenthia, C.D., T.T. - 1975

August

August makes me nervous.
The days begin to shorten
and katydids chirp of autumn.

Three of my dearest collies died
In this eighth month:
Lady,
  Cindy,
    Kieno.
They've left gaps in my heart
that I've never filled.

Amber is my oldest collie,
a joint gift from my husband to me
when we married.
I paid for her
as I was to pay for nearly everything
throughout the marriage.
Our attempts to breed her were futile,
like my dreams of loving someone forever.

Serena came six years later.
I had grand plans to breed her.
instead, she pushed us further apart
running away from my husband
every chance she got.
I was too blind
to understand why.

Then, on the anniversary
of Lady's demise,
my marriage ended.

It is a year after the divorce
and now it's August again.
Amber lies in scorching sun

Kieno I described as: "the collie with a face of
gold and a heart to match." – 1975

that soothes her stiff haunches.
She is happy with the serenity
of our single household.
Even Serena has calmed down.
Since my husband left,
she no longer runs away.

Last month, Julie came
a rescue collie
hungry for affection
grateful to belong.
How could I refuse
when I had the space
and love
to give her?

Karen holding puppies from first litter. Left to right: Karenthia's
Tartan Tryst, C.D., Karenthia's Tartan Tapestry, Karenthia's Tartan
Thistle. On the ground: Cindy – Carwill's Witch of Karenthia,
C.D., T.T. and Karenthia's Tartan Tinker, C.D. - 1976

Paw Prints

Metal paw print
hangs from the car mirror
and leads the way
as my dogs have always
led the way in my life.

My breath in sync with theirs,
they are my compass,
my internal clock.

Always the dogs.
Always their lessons.
No matter how many years,
no matter how many dogs,
always there is a new gleaning.

I look into the amber depths
of their eyes and see
my soul reflected there,
paw prints on my heart.

Talking to God

It is bitter cold.
The labyrinth is on a canvas mat
at the back of our room.
It is quiet. Everyone is sewing.
We are encouraged
to walk the labyrinth
at our own pace
in our own time.

Before I begin I stop
shut my eyes,
take a deep breath.
"Let me know God," I pray.

I enter the labyrinth
in stocking feet,
turning left then right
back and forth
around and around the turns.
My arms tingle.
I feel the familiar alignment.

I reach the center,
alone,
I pause,
take another deep breath.
As I walk out
God speaks to me:

"You know me
through the unconditional love
of your dogs.
I have always
been with you,
as your dogs
have always
been with you,

loving and protecting you.
You have seen me reflected
in their eyes.
You have felt me
in the unbearable sorrow
of their passing.
I have always been with you."

Karen holding Karenthia's Terra-Cotta, C.D.,H.C. (age 12 weeks) –
1986. Terra is a daughter of Splash and littersister of Travis.

My Blessing

Collies are my blessing.
I have lived with them every day
for the last fifty years.
In their eyes is forgiveness,
in their wagging tails, laughter.
They are my daily prayer.
They listen to my confession.
Stroking their fur is my rosary.
Nothing in my life has touched my soul
as much as my beloved collies.
What is it about their expression
that takes my breath away?
I don't know why I love them so.
They have raised me from childhood
listened to my woes and my worries,
forgiven my trespasses
patiently nudged me in the right direction.
They have shown me
all that is good and kind
all that I am or hope to be.
Reflected in their eyes
I see the person God sees:
perfect in my imperfection.
That is how my collies look at me every day.
It is heady stuff yet humbling
as a whispered prayer
in the dark of night.
In this world I count myself wealthy
with all the wonderful dogs I've had.
By that tally,
I am richer than Solomon.

Bobby – Tartan's Tri Spook of Karenthia - 1969

Breaking

Nothing has opened my heart
like the collies I have shown
and bred and loved
for fifty years.
Show dogs that didn't turn out,
winners who couldn't be bred.
A continuing parade of dogs
who stayed for a short time
or for their entire lives.
Over and over hopes dashed
while pursuing the ideal collie.
Some dogs were easier to let go,
others it was torture to part with.
For some, an untimely death ended
my hopes and dreams.
Bobby, Cindy, Kieno, Amber, Serena,
the list goes on.
Always the dogs.
Always their wisdom guiding me,
their brave hearts protecting me,
their happy faces making me laugh.
My life and theirs have been
entwined since childhood.
Nothing has brought me more joy
or heartbreaking sorrow
the way my dogs have.
A divorce?
The death of my father?
Cancer?
They all pale besides the
gut wrenching heartache
of loss sustained
with my beloved collies.
It's as if someone reached into my chest
pulled out my heart, broke it,
then pushed it back in.

Karenthia's Travis MGee, C.D., H.C. - 1988. Travis is a
son of Splash and litterbrother of Terra-Cotta.

Maybe that's the secret of living:
to break your heart
again and again
until it stays open
forever.

Karen and Lady on beach at Sherwood Island in Westport, Connecticut – 1972

Sacred Space

In sacred space
Lady sits beside me
beaming with love,
smiling with joy.

Looking at her
makes me feel
happy, centered, and safe.
She is my soul mother,
a part of my heart.

Her wisdom reaches
beyond the stars.
She knows all things
in this world
and in others.

Eloquent beyond words,
beautiful beyond inspiration.

She guides me.
She consoles me.
She praises me.
Her voice
is the song of my heart.

My Saddle

My Hartley saddle
sits in a corner of the living room
on a special aluminum stand.
I can't let go of my dream.
Even after I buy my house,
change jobs, gain weight,
and collies become my life,
I still dream of riding and
keep my custom boots.

I fuel my love of horses with films:
The Black Stallion, Seabiscuit, Secretariat;
and books: *Blue Rodeo, Shadow Ranch,*
Riding Lessons, Flying Changes.

Then new neighbors build a paddock
and their horses come to the fence.
Lady Hawk, a demanding pinto mare,
and Sundance, her sorrel companion.
I look for them and
feed them apples.

My saddle stands guard
through marriage,
the house renovation,
divorce,
the death of my father.
For thirty years it keeps me company
takes up valuable space.

Then one day I let it go,
donate my saddle to Pegasus,
a program that enables
handicapped children
to ride horses.

I pass along my love of riding

through my saddle.
It feels right.

I still love horses,
I always will.

I loved them first.

About the Author

Karen Phelps, MA, is a, award-winning writer, editor, photographer, and quilter. Karenthia, her kennel, has won many awards in the four decades breeding and showing pure-bred collies. She is a native of Westchester County, New York where she lives with her two dogs and cat, Ginger.

Printed in the United States
By Bookmasters